HEALING FROM
BROKENNESS

women of faith™

HEALING FROM BROKENNESS

BY

KIM STONE

FOREWORD BY

SHEILA WALSH

THOMAS NELSON
Since 1798

Published in Nashville, Tennessee, by Thomas Nelson. Thomas Nelson is a registered trademark of HarperCollins Christian Publishing, Inc.

Thomas Nelson titles may be purchased in bulk for educational, business, fund-raising, or sales promotional use. For information, please e-mail SpecialMarkets@ ThomasNelson.com.

Unless otherwise noted, Scripture quotations are taken from *The Holy Bible*, The New King James Version (NKJV®). © 1979, 1980, 1982, by Thomas Nelson. Used by permission. All rights reserved.

Scripture quotations marked NCV are taken from the *New Century Version*®. © 2005 by Thomas Nelson. Used by permission. All rights reserved.

Scripture quotations marked NIV are taken from *The Holy Bible*, New International Version®. NIV®. © 1973, 1978, 1984, 2011 by Biblica, Inc.® Used by permission. All rights reserved.

ISBN-13: 978-0-310-68253-0

HB 04.08.2024

☝ Contents ☝

FOREWORD

I watched as the radio interviewer shook his head. He was reading messages posted onto a monitor in front of him by the producer of his show. In a sentence or two he was being told about incoming calls and the questions the listeners wanted to ask.

"Is that a tough question?" I asked.

"It's too personal," he said. "The caller wants to ask about your time in a psychiatric hospital."

"I'll be very happy to take the call," I said, and so he put her through.

"Is it true that you spent a month in a psychiatric hospital?" she asked.

"It is," I said. "I was hospitalized with severe clinical depression."

"Did you feel as if your life was over?" she asked.

"I did. It was the scariest time in my life," I told her. "Even though at the beginning it seemed to me that my life was over, I discovered that because of the love and mercy of God, it was really just a new beginning. Facing the truth is hard but it is also very liberating."

"I've been struggling with depression for over two years," she said, "but I am too ashamed to get help. I feel as if I'm letting God down."

"I understand how you feel," I said, "I felt that, too, until I began to comprehend the depth of God's compassion. He loves us right now, just as we are, and he longs for us to bring your brokenness to him so that he can heal us."

"I want the pain to just go away," she whispered. "I don't think I have the strength to face everything that has happened in my past."

"You don't on your own," I agreed, "but you are not alone."

How well I understood this dear sister's aching heart. I, too, have found myself at the edge of a dark night afraid to take one more step in case the darkness overwhelmed me. I have tried to push painful memories into the most hidden room of my heart and simply move on with my life. What I discovered, though, is that when we close off our heart to pain, we close it off to the love and light of God as well.

I don't know what brokenness you are facing or what caused you to pick up this study guide, but I want to encourage you that you are embarking on an amazing adventure of freedom and grace. No matter how fragile you feel, let me remind you of the words of the prophet Isaiah as he spoke of the coming

Messiah, "He will not break a crushed blade of grass or put out even a weak flame" (Isaiah 42:3 NCV).

It is my sincere prayer that when you have completed this study, you will know an internal liberty that you have never known before. God bless you, my sister!

—*Sheila Walsh*

⚐ INTRODUCTION ⚑

My sacrifice, O God, is a broken spirit; a broken and contrite heart you, God, will not despise.

Psalm 5:17, NIV

We were sitting in the dim and quiet living room, nursing our babies. I don't remember where our husbands and the older children were—probably outside. But I do remember my friend's sweet face as she confided to me, "I know you don't really want to know about this stuff, but you need to. I was molested as a child, and I want you to help me work through this."

She wondered if I would be shocked, repulsed, but all I felt was a well of compassion, such love and such humbleness that she would be willing to share the dark as well as the bright side of life with me.

Maybe not all of us have dealt with an event in our past that has been this traumatic. But each and every one of us has had an experience that has left us broken, an experience that has forced us to cry out for help. Maybe it was a divorce or bankruptcy, a severe car accident or the death of a close friend or relative, a life-threatening illness or a battle with depression. However unique your personal experience with brokenness has been, each and every one of us has dealt with the same emotions, empty-heartedness, and doubt. We have all been there.

But do you know why this is good news? You are surrounded by sisters who can share your tears and cheer you on to true wholeness. We have all been disappointed in people, events, and maybe even what God has allowed to happen. But despite our doubts, we have a Savior who understands brokenheartedness and who is orchestrating every minute detail of our lives. Remember when Jesus was weeping over Jerusalem? He said, "How often I wanted to gather your children together, as a hen gathers her chicks under her wings, but you were not willing!" (Matthew 23:37). By beginning this study, we are saying that we are willing for Jesus to gather us under His wings. There is no safer refuge, and like a mother hen, He is willing to die to protect His chicks. With an advocate like that, what is there to fear?

The book of Jude ends with some of my favorite verses in the Bible: "To him who is able to keep you from falling and to present you before his glorious presence without fault and with great joy—to the only God our Savior be glory, majesty, power and authority, through Jesus Christ our Lord, before all ages, now and forevermore" (Jude 1:24 NIV). The fact that Jesus can keep me from falling, and not only that, He can present me without fault and with great joy, tells me three things. I don't have to repeat the events of my past. I can live without sin with regard to those events. There can be great joy in my life.

As for my friend who began her own journey to healing on that long-ago day, we spent that autumn with a few other women, talking and praying about life and hard events. We didn't solve all of the problems, but we loved each other and retain those bonds to this day. That is my prayer for those of you who share in this study: that you will love one another, pray together, and cheer each other on to a life of joy, because Jesus came into the world to give us just that.

Have you not known?
Have you not heard?
The everlasting God, the LORD,
The Creator of the ends of the earth,
Never faints nor is weary.
His understanding is unsearchable.
He gives power to the weak,
And to those who have no might He increases strength.
Even the youths shall faint and be weary,
And the young men shall utterly fall,
But those who wait on the LORD
Shall renew their strength;
They shall mount up with wings like eagles,
They shall run and not be weary,
They shall walk and not faint."

Isaiah 40:28–31

CHAPTER ONE

A Broken World

For all have sinned and fall short
of the glory of God.

—Romans 3:23

hen you turned on the news this morning, what did you hear? Was the television station broadcasting all fuzzy, feel-good stories, or were there plenty of unpleasant stories, as well? I don't know about you, but every time I turn on the TV, I hear bad news. Headlines scream of murder, war, corrupt politicians, drugs, robbery, child abuse. There is no shortage of bad news. And it's not just on the TV screen, newspaper, talk shows, or published biographies of people who have gone through tough times. We don't have to look far within our own circle of friends to find someone whose life has been touched by bad news. Perhaps it was even our own.

It's not such a stretch to realize that we live in a broken world, and we are all products of its depravity. Each and every one of us has not only dealt with the repercussions of people's bad actions, but if we look inward at ourselves we can see that it's not always other people who are to blame.

CLEARING ⚹ THE ⚹ COBWEBS

The truth is, we live in a broken world, and we are all products of its depravity. Each and every one of us has not only dealt with the repercussions of people's bad actions, but if we look inward at ourselves, we can see that it's not always other people who are to blame.

Orpah was born to two unmarried teenagers in the poverty-stricken countryside of Kosciusko, Mississippi. Unable to support their daughter, her parents sent her to live with various family members at different times in her younger years. At the age of nine, Orpah was molested by several of her male relatives. Instead of telling anyone, she funneled her hurt and anger into rebellious actions, including drug use and promiscuity. By the time she was fourteen, Orpah gave birth to a premature little boy who died after childbirth.

As she was holding her dead child, fourteen-year-old Orpah decided to turn her life around. She vowed that she would do everything in her power to find freedom from the cycle of sin and destruction that she had been caught in for so long. She excelled at her studies, won the Miss Black Tennessee beauty pageant, and became the first black female news anchor in Nashville, Tennessee. From there, she went on to host her own television show, win Golden Globes and Emmys, launch her own magazine, open several charitable organizations (including a school for girls in South Africa), and be named as one of the world's most influential women. This young woman, born as Orpah, now has one of the most well-known names in the world—Oprah Winfrey.

Oprah has influenced our culture and changed countless lives with her inspirational story and benevolent spirit. Imagine if she had allowed her past—the poverty, the abuse, and her own bad choices—to define what she could do with her life! Not only would she have missed out on all God had planned for her, but so many people would have been left unchanged.

1. Have you ever seen people who let their pasts negatively dictate choices they have made for their future? Explain.

2. As we begin this study, take an assessment of your life. Was there an event in your past that dramatically influenced how you interact with the world? Do you feel broken and needy or restored and complete? Are you ready to find all the good God has in store for your life?

Everyone has a past, a history of sin that has left our lives broken. The truth is, because of Adam and Eve's long-ago choice to defy God, we were born into their sinful legacy. We have all done things that are wrong, and have had wrong things done to us. And the repercussions are not always easy to shrug off. Maybe our past is not biography-worthy like Oprah's, but independent of whether we came from poverty and abuse or privilege and love, we are still sinful humans in need of a Savior.

A Samaritan woman was confronted by her past one day as she went into the city to draw water from a well. As she was drawing her water, a stranger spoke to her and asked her for a drink. Read John's account of this interaction in John 4:4–38.

3. You can picture this woman speaking to the stranger, hoping against hope that He didn't know anything about her circumstances. Little did she know she was speaking with Jesus, who knows every detail about each of our lives. What did Jesus tell this woman about her past? What would He be able to tell you about your past?

4. In verses 28–30, what did the woman say and do? How do her actions indicate that she had finally come to recognize Jesus as the Messiah?

5. Throughout their conversation, the woman insisted on taking every-thing Jesus said literally, while Jesus tried to help her see His true mean-ing behind His words. In the space below, list both the literal meanings and the spiritual translations of the things they talked about.

6. Just like the Samaritan woman, have you ever felt so blinded by your circumstances that you have been unable to see God in your life? Explain.

Like the Samaritan woman who had trouble looking past her circumstances to recognize Jesus as the Messiah, sometimes we have trouble seeing God in the midst of our broken world, especially a caring and loving God. But the truth is that God does love us and will restore us if only we trust in Him. The Bible is brimming with stories of redemption. From Mary Magdalene to Paul, we can see how God uses broken sinners from the most unlikely circumstances to bring about changes in their lives and the lives of others.

7. Do you believe God can restore your broken past and make you whole again? Is there anything from your past that you believe is too big for Him to handle? Explain.

8. When you think about your future, what kind of plans do you think God has in store for you? Read *Jeremiah 29:11*. Whenever you begin to doubt your future, remember this verse.

DIGGING DEEPER

There is a lot of hurt and brokenness in our world, but it does not always come about in a dramatic form. Sometimes long-lasting hurt can come from something as simple as a parent working all the time instead of spending time with their child, or children teasing each other on the playground. Think about the different forms of brokenness, and how it all relates back to Romans 3:23: "For all have sinned and fall short of the glory of God."

PONDER & PRAY

Take a moment to think about your life from God's perspective. Do you think He likes the way you see yourself? The way you conduct yourself? The hope you have in your future? Pray through Jeremiah 29:11 and ask God to allow you to start looking at your life from His perspective.

TRINKETS TO TREASURE

At the close of each lesson, you will be presented with a small gift. Though imaginary, it will serve to remind you of the things you have learned. Think of it as a souvenir! Souvenirs are little trinkets we pick up on our journeys to remind us of where we have been. They keep us from forgetting the path we have travelled. Hide these little treasures in your heart, for as you ponder on them, they will draw you closer to God!

Our gift for this week is a journal, to help remind us to start keeping a record of our progress. After each lesson, write a few sentences to help you remember what you've learned and how far you've come. Believe me, we have an exciting road ahead of us, and you're not going to want to miss it!

NOTES & PRAYER REQUESTS

CHAPTER TWO

ADOPTED BY GOD

BUT AS MANY AS RECEIVED HIM, TO THEM HE
GAVE THE RIGHT TO BECOME CHILDREN OF GOD,
TO THOSE WHO BELIEVE IN HIS NAME: WHO WERE
BORN, NOT OF BLOOD, NOR OF THE WILL OF THE
FLESH, NOR OF THE WILL OF MAN, BUT OF GOD.

—John 1:12–13

Some friends of ours recently adopted a group of siblings from war-torn Liberia. Given away by their mother who couldn't support them, these children were in need of love, peace, stability—in short, these children needed a home.

"How's it going?" I asked my friend after she had had the children for a few weeks.

"Margie, I could have borne these children. They fit into our family like they have always been here," she replied. Then she laughed gently as she remembered some of their adjustments, and went on to say soberly, "People act like we have done something so wonderful or self-sacrificing to adopt these children, but it's not like that. We are the ones who have been blessed. God gave them to us, and it has been such a gift."

Despite her attempt to downplay her actions, my friend had done something extraordinary. She found three children who had never known love,

CLEARING THE COBWEBS

The truth is that He loves each one of us as a person, no matter what we have done or what has happened to us. He made you, He willingly paid for you through Jesus' death, and He wants to see your face at our family reunion in heaven along with the rest of His adopted children.

plucked them out of their broken world, and vowed to love them unconditionally. She didn't need to do this. But she wanted to. And she was blessed by it.

God yearns to adopt each one of us, bringing us out of our broken pasts and showering us with freedom and love. Adoption is the center of God's heart because He knows that each of us needs to be adopted by Him, even if we feel we don't deserve it. No matter how good or bad our childhood family was, we are each like those children from war-torn Liberia whose mother could not support them. There is something missing that needs to be provided. Every human being is born with the need to know and understand God, and like little children, we have to be raised, trained, and taught how to fit into God's family.

But as much as we would like it to be, this is not an automatic occurrence. Jesus explained that being born again means first believing in Him. He says, "For God so loved the world that He gave His only begotten Son, that whoever believes in Him should not perish but have everlasting life" (John 3:16).

There are two very important points in this well-known and well-loved verse: God willingly gave His Son for us, hence we are born again because God wants us to be; and God loves us. It is not just that God loves the rest of the world and He got stuck with you and me along with the rest. He loves each one of us as a person, no matter what we have done or what has happened to us.

He made you, He willingly paid for you through Jesus' death, and He wants to see your face at our family reunion in heaven along with the rest of His adopted children. But first you must believe in Him as your Father.

1. Do you know anyone who has been adopted or who has adopted a child? What was their experience like? How is this experience like what God wants for us?

2. Even though God wants to adopt all of us, the first step is in our hands. Have you ever taken this first step toward becoming a child of God? If not, what is holding you back? If so, what has your experience been?

Read Ephesians 1:3–8. This passage has traditionally been labeled as slightly controversial due to the questions it brings up about predestination, but try to look past this smaller issue in order to grasp the big picture of what Paul is saying: "He predestined us to be adopted as his sons through Jesus Christ, in accordance with his pleasure and will" (NIV).

3. In your own words, what is the "big picture" of what Paul is saying in this passage?

4. Notice the verb Paul used in verse 4—*chose*. How does this word underscore God's desire for us to be His children?

5. How does the timing of when He chose us emphasize the plans God has for you?

You are not an afterthought! God has known about you since before the world began, and He takes pleasure in the idea of adopting you as His child!

6. Read *Romans 8:12–16*. What does *verse 14* say about how to recognize a son (and a daughter!) of God?

In Ephesians 5:13–14, Paul tells us that as sons and daughters of God, we have been marked with the Holy Spirit to seal our adoption, so to speak. In Romans 8:15, he goes on to say that this very same Spirit does not make us slaves to fear, but allows us to live freely as children of God.

7. As we are talking about our broken pasts, how does the promise given in *Romans 8:15* resonate with you? How does it give you freedom to move on without fear?

We will be exploring this concept of freedom more in the following lesson, but for now just revel in the truth that God loves you as His child, no matter where you came from or what you have done—and He has loved you this way since before the world began!

DIGGING DEEPER

Read Psalm 139. How does this psalm reinforce the idea that God has been involved in our lives from the very beginning? Reading David's words of praise, is it such a stretch to think that God wants us as His children? That He has been with us through the darker and the lighter times of life? That He has a plan for us?

PONDER & PRAY

Read 1 John 4:7. Take a moment to meditate on what it means to be "born of God." Thank God for snatching you away from your broken past and adopting you into His family. If you are in a group, take a moment to share your thoughts on being born of God. Pray, thanking your Father for His never-ending love and mercy.

TRINKETS TO TREASURE

This week's token is a reminder that all believers in Christ have been adopted into God's family. To bring this home this week, think of a way you can touch the life of an orphan. Maybe it's through volunteering at an orphanage, writing a letter, sponsoring a child (there are many different organizations from which you can choose), or even considering adopting a child yourself. Whatever it is, think of a way you can be a blessing to a child who may not have been fortunate enough to have the love of a family.

NOTES & PRAYER REQUESTS

CHAPTER THREE

FREE INDEED

JESUS REPLIED, "I TELL YOU THE TRUTH, EVERYONE
WHO SINS IS A SLAVE TO SIN. NOW A SLAVE HAS
NO PERMANENT PLACE IN THE FAMILY, BUT A SON
BELONGS TO IT FOREVER. SO IF THE SON SETS YOU
FREE, YOU WILL BE FREE INDEED."

—John 8:34–36, NIV

On an early spring day in 1984, a young man stopped by our house to pick up his mandolin, which my husband had repaired. It wasn't convenient timing. My husband had come home from the hospital that morning following his second cancer surgery, and we were still adjusting not only to the business of pain medication and nursing care, but the cataclysmic impact that cancer has on a young family. But I sensed the Lord nudging me, so we said, "Sure, come on over." He arrived on his bike with a backpack, and while he was stuffing his instrument into the top of his pack, he explained that he had sold all of his stuff and was moving over the mountains to a certain remote area where, as he described it, he hoped to be free.

"Do you want to know how to be really free?" I asked him.

He looked up at me, rather startled. "Yes."

So I told him about Jesus, who died on the

CLEARING ⇗ THE ⇖ COBWEBS

The truth is that we may have one sin acting as the biggest obstacle to freedom, the simplest sin we didn't even notice — thinking that our past is too overwhelming for God to do anything about.

cross for our sins, who came to this earth to set us free. When we ask Him to save us, I told the young man, He makes us free to be the person He created us to be.

Still kneeling on the porch where he had been struggling into his pack, Pat prayed for Jesus to forgive him and come into his life. And then he went leaping across the lawn, backpack lurching crazily, shouting, "I'm free, I'm free!" We knew we would probably never see him again, but we would pray for him, and his Savior and ours would never let him out of sight.

There is something so alluring about freedom. It may conjure up images of endless beaches under a sunny sky, tramping the trails in the high country, or just sleeping in. In one way or another, we envision a life without hassles. But the kind of freedom that Christ promises is to be free from the fruits of sin.

It is one thing to understand that God has accepted us, but it's another thing entirely to be set free by this realization. Without our knowledge, we may have one sin acting as the biggest obstacle to freedom, the simplest sin we don't even notice—thinking that our past is too overwhelming for God to do anything about. Without even knowing it, we are cutting ourselves off from God's power, and we are effectively closing the door to healing.

When you are free in Christ, it means that you don't have to dread Mother's Day because you had an abortion when you were young. It means that you can raise your little boys to be godly men even if your husband abandoned you. It means you can look at a bottle of alcohol, a box of cigarettes, or even a plate of cookies and realize those things no longer have any power over you. It means that you can love the unlovely, because Christ first loved you. It means that you are free to be a giver because you are no longer shackled by your past.

The Bible is full of real people who experienced the messiest parts of life, and who also found that in the midst of their turmoil, God cared for them, before they even knew how to cry out. The woman caught in adultery is one of these.

1. Read John 8:1–11. How do you think the woman in this passage felt? Spend some time thinking about how it would feel to be in the middle of a group of accusers, and make a list of emotions she might have had. Look at your list. Have you ever felt this way about your own past?

2. Notice Jesus' first response. Why did He first take a step back from the accusers by kneeling down on the ground?

3. What is the significance of Jesus' comment to the accusers?

4. What did Jesus tell the woman? Does His response mean He thought that adultery didn't matter? What does it tell us about Jesus' attitude toward the woman? Toward her sin?

5. Even though there's no way of knowing, what do you suppose the woman did next?

The story of the woman caught in adultery shows us that no matter how messy our past has been, Jesus still offers us His forgiveness. In fact, Jesus' whole purpose for coming to earth was to set us free.

6. Read John 8:31–36. What did Jesus mean when He talked about being "set free"?

7. Just exactly what is the truth that sets us free? (You may want to read John 1:1–18 and John 3:1–21.)

8. What does it mean to be a slave to sin? What is the difference between a son and a slave?

9. How can you act like a son (or daughter) of God instead of a slave to sin? What would this look like in your life? In the space below, write a few practical ways in which you can change your day-to-day life to reflect your status as God's child.

Digging Deeper

Accepting that we are free from our past means that we are also free from human judgments regarding our past. Just like the adulterous woman, we are no longer accountable to our accusers, but only to God. Read Galatians 5:1–15. Consider what it means to no longer be justified by law but to be free in Christ. How does this change the way you think of your past? How does this change the way you view your future?

Ponder & Pray

Take a few minutes to thank God for setting you free from your past sins. Ask Him to help you truly accept His freedom and live as one of His children, not as a slave to sin. Tell Him about any areas of your life in which you still feel trapped by your sin. Maybe you are still dealing with the repercussions, so it is hard for you to feel free. Or perhaps you feel judged by others because of things that have happened in your past. Ask God to help you move past these things so you can claim the freedom He died to give you.

Trinkets To Treasure

This week's token is a reminder to take an assessment of our lives. What are some ways in which we still act like a slave to sin? Do we still feel entrapped by our past sins? Can we see the repercussions of those sins in our everyday lives? Memorize Galatians 5:1 and claim it every time you are reminded of your sin. Write it out and tape it to your bathroom mirror so you will see it every morning when you wake up and every evening before going to bed.

NOTES & PRAYER REQUESTS

CHAPTER FOUR

Under His Wings

HE SHALL COVER YOU WITH HIS FEATHERS,
AND UNDER HIS WINGS YOU SHALL TAKE REFUGE;
HIS TRUTH SHALL BE YOUR SHIELD AND BUCKLER.

—Psalm 91:4

Do you remember learning to do the back float? The swimming instructor would say, "Relax! The water will hold you up," and I would think, *What do you mean, "relax"? I'll go straight to the bottom with my nose full of water!* But I lay on my back, believing only that a transparent-looking substance would be strong enough to hold me up, and that possibly, if my swimming instructor took pity on me, I would have helping hands to catch me if things went south.

Learning to rest in the Lord is a little like learning to swim. Certain facts about swimming and water help, but nothing takes the place of practice. As a Christian, it is often when we find ourselves in deep, uncharted waters that we get this practice, for it is these deep-water experiences of life that force us to learn to trust completely in the Lord. Death, divorce, the lives of our children suddenly collapsing, betrayal of trust,

CLEARING ⫦ THE ⫧ COBWEBS

The truth is that while God hasn't promised we will lead lives free of suffering, He will be with us through every trial we endure.

relationships gone awry for reasons we don't really understand, childhood traumas catching up with us, are all events that pitch us out of our comfort zones into the murky uncertainties that cause us to question ourselves, our God, and our expectations of what life should be like.

Though God allows us to go through these deep-water experiences, He never leaves our side. Just like the swimming instructor who was ready to catch us when we began to sink, God is there, not to remove the waves and the storms, but to guide us through them and protect us along the way.

Elijah experienced the rest and provision of the Lord in his flight from Queen Jezebel, who wanted him dead. In 1 Kings 18 Elijah had just called down fire from heaven to consume the sacrifice to the Lord and confound the prophets of Baal. It had been a spectacular defeat of those false prophets and a triumphant demonstration of the power of God. Yet in the very next chapter Elijah is found running for his life!

As Elijah was fleeing, he sat under a tree and begged God for death. The Lord didn't comfort him, or give him a pep talk. He sent an angel with something to eat. Twice. The angel said, "Arise and eat, because the journey is too great for you" (1 Kings 19:7).

This story is a classic case of the question, "Why do bad things happen to good people?" Elijah had just done the Lord's will by defeating the false prophets, but it only served to intensify Queen Jezebel's wrath and put Elijah at risk of death. But right when Elijah was ready to give up, the Lord came through with exactly what Elijah needed—food and rest.

That is what resting in the Lord is all about. It means letting God nourish you when the journey is too great for you to walk alone. It is about coming to the end of your rope and realizing that God is still there to meet you and push you just a little farther. It is about keeping your eyes on Him and trusting that no matter what, He will never let you sink beneath the waves into the deep waters.

God has promised that He will not give us more than we can bear (1 Corinthians 10:13) and that He will help us in times of trouble (Psalm 46). Psalm 22 starts out with heart cries of anguish, and ends with praise to the Lord. There is great comfort in telling the Lord all about our troubles, and comfort, too, in remembering His promises of tender care for us.

1. Have you ever been at a point where you felt like you couldn't go on? Did you try telling God about it? How did it make you feel telling your problems to Someone who is capable of handling them?

2. Read Psalm 23. What is the job of the shepherd? How does this aspect of God's character make you trust Him more?

3. Considering your present circumstances, what would be a green pasture that would give you rest? What would restore your soul?

4. What represents the Lord's rod and staff to you?

5. What is your favorite promise from the last two verses of Psalm 23? Why do these words especially speak to you?

God not only gives us comfort, but He also protects us from our enemies. Psalm 91 tells of God's watchful care for us.

6. Read this psalm. What do you think it means to dwell in the secret place of the Most High? What would this look like in your life?

7. Have you ever felt not just overwhelmed by your problems, but afraid of them? How does this passage give you courage?

8. This psalm is full of encouraging words and wonderful promises. Which verse speaks most clearly to you and why? Write it down on a note card and carry it with you throughout the week.

When you are feeling anxious and weary, praise God for everything you can think of. Start with your own salvation and Christ's willingness to be your Savior. You will be reminded of the mercy Christ has had on you, and that God has always had a plan for your life. Even out of pain and sorrow He can bring joy and victory.

DIGGING DEEPER

Psalm 91 tells us, "Because you have made the LORD, who is my refuge, even the Most High, your dwelling place, no evil shall befall you, nor shall any plague come near your dwelling; for He shall give His angels charge over you, to keep you in all your ways" (verses 9–11). Maybe you have been a victim of the sins of others. Perhaps this has even contributed to your broken past. In the midst of dealing with the repercussions of evil in your life, these verses may sound hollow. How have you seen the Lord take care of you during your trouble? How can you hide in Him when you still don't have the answer to all of your questions?

PONDER & PRAY

In 1 Corinthians 10:13, the Bible says that God will never give us more than we can handle. Spend a few minutes thinking back over your past and thanking God for bringing you this far. Think of one blessing that has come out of your trials and praise Him for it. If you are in a group, take turns praising the Lord for the simplest thing He has done for you this week. Perhaps it was helping you find your lost car keys, or giving you a moment of peace during a hectic day. Whatever it is, let it remind you that God cares for even the smallest problems you face.

TRINKETS TO TREASURE

This week's token is a reminder to begin making a list of times when God has given you rest and provision in the midst of problems. Maybe it was a neighbor bringing over a casserole when a parent died, or a friend bringing over cookie dough and a movie to take your mind off a breakup, or even just a beautiful sunset that seemed to be painted just for you. As the week goes on, you will probably recall more and more times when God has given you a little boost to keep you going, Write them down and be encouraged next time something goes wrong.

NOTES & PRAYER REQUESTS

CHAPTER FIVE

THE BUCK STOPS HERE

DO NOT BE OVERCOME BY EVIL, BUT OVERCOME EVIL WITH GOOD.

—Romans 12:21

Have you ever surprised yourself by saying something that sounds just like your mother? Or have you ever told your husband that he's acting like his father? We all inherit traits from our parents, whether we realize it or not. Some are good, and some are bad; some are desirable, and some are destructive.

But how many times have we blamed our adult troubles on our families? Perhaps we blame our mounting debt on the poor spending habits our parents modeled. Maybe we have trouble controlling our temper because our parents were always yelling at each other and us. Or perhaps we blame our alcoholism on the genes passed down to us.

Whatever the circumstances, the buck stops here. We must all take responsibility for the situations in which we find ourselves and refuse to continue indulging our sinful natures because of

CLEARING ⚐ THE ⚐ COBWEBS

The truth is that we must make the conscious decision to change in order to keep from passing on the same legacy of pain and sin that was given to us.

our past. Even more important, we must make the conscious decision to change in order to keep from passing on the same legacy of pain and sin that was given to us.

God means for us to seek ways to mend the holes from the past and to learn to do things His way. We won't be perfect. We won't catch everything. But we can make a start. And the next generation can do a little better. My friend Elaine had some hard times with her mother. "I try not to pass those things on to my children," she says soberly. And then she adds with a twinkle in her eye, "I can make plenty of mistakes on my own!"

It takes a lot of work to find freedom from a broken past—the same past that we want to throw away and never think of again. If we really want to be sure that we don't pass things on, we have to do some serious thinking not only about what happened, but about how we responded, what could be better about our response, and whether we even know what a right response might be.

Consider the story of Joseph and his brothers. This is probably one of the best illustrations of replacing a legacy of sin with one of forgiveness and renewal.

1. Read Genesis 37. Why were Joseph's brothers jealous of him? How would you respond if you were told by someone you were jealous of that he or she would one day rule over you?

2. What did Joseph's brothers decide to do to Joseph? What were the different reactions to Joseph's disappearance?

Joseph's story continues in Potiphar's household, and then in prison when he refused the advances of Potiphar's wife.

3. Read Genesis 39:1–6 and 20–23. Joseph could have wasted his time feeling sorry for himself, developing a bitter hatred toward the Egyptians who had bought him, or plotting to kill his brothers if he ever had the opportunity. What did Joseph do instead? How did the Lord bless him?

Before long, Pharaoh required Joseph's dream-interpretation skills and summoned him from prison. Again the Lord was with Joseph, and he was able to interpret Pharaoh's dream, which told him that the land would experience seven years of plenty and seven years of famine. Pharaoh was so impressed with Joseph's wisdom that he placed him in charge of the kingdom of Egypt as his second-in-command.

When the famine struck, Joseph's brothers traveled to Egypt to buy food for their family. When they knelt before Joseph to request food, Joseph recognized his brothers—the same ones who had sold him into slavery so many years before.

4. Read Genesis 45 to see how Joseph finally revealed his identity to his brothers. What was the brothers' reaction when they found out the ruler over Egypt was the same brother whom they had sold into slavery? What did Joseph say to appease their fears?

5. How was Joseph's response to his brothers the same or different from how you would have reacted? How did Joseph's outlook on his situation indicate his belief that God brings good out of evil situations?

6. Make a list of all the good things Joseph did for his brothers.

Joseph truly repaid evil deeds with good. Even though he was in a position where he could have caused his family much pain and suffering, he chose to give them every good thing he could think of instead of retaliating.

7. Read Romans 12:17–20. How does this response seem counterintuitive to the way we might want to respond to our enemies? But how is it effective in terminating the cycle of sin in which we might find ourselves?

8. Is there anyone with whom you need to live at peace instead of harboring vengeful thoughts toward? What is something you could do to feed or clothe your enemy, so to speak?

The bottom line is that sin is expensive. Whether we are the ones who have been broken by others' sinful behavior, or whether it is our own choices that have wounded us and others, the answer is still the same. Our Lord wants us to be free from the consequences of sin. We are, every one of us, "damaged goods" in need of restoration. As we are restored, we can become sure that we will not pass on the consequences of our pain—that we will be good parents, family members, and friends; that we will be able to face life without fear, anxiety, bitterness, and shame.

DIGGING DEEPER

We always have a choice—the choice to allow God to change our hearts, or to hold on to the way we have always done things. While we have no control over the hearts of others, we can love them. Read Romans 12:9–21. How would living out this passage change the way you act toward others? How could it possibly change others' hearts?

Ponder & Pray

Pray that you will know how to love your enemies. Pray for any reconciliation that may need to take place. Spend some time this week praying for friends or relatives, that they will see the attitudes of their own hearts and that the Lord will show them if there are areas that need to change.

Trinkets to Treasure

This week's token is a reminder to reach out to someone in forgiveness like Joseph reached out to his brothers. Write a letter to someone whom you have formerly blamed for your problems. Maybe they deserved your blame or maybe they didn't, but whatever the situation, write them a letter telling them that you forgive them. If you do not feel ready to send the letter yet, keep it until you do.

NOTES & PRAYER REQUESTS

CHAPTER SIX

FORGIVE WITH BOTH HANDS

THEN PETER CAME TO HIM AND SAID, "LORD, HOW OFTEN
SHALL MY BROTHER SIN AGAINST ME, AND I FORGIVE
HIM . . . ?" JESUS SAID TO HIM, "I DO NOT SAY TO YOU,
UP TO SEVEN TIMES, BUT UP TO SEVENTY TIMES SEVEN."

—Matthew 18:21–22

 veryone, no matter who you are, has been wronged at some point in life. Once wronged, the question remains: "Will I forgive? *Can* I forgive?"

It has been said that Spanish Prime Minister Ramón María Narváez requested a priest on his deathbed. "Does your Excellency forgive all your enemies?" the priest asked. "I do not have to forgive my enemies," Narváez retorted. "I have had them all shot." While this is clearly not a healthy reaction, it does seem a whole lot easier than figuring out how we can possibly forgive someone who has wronged us!

Forgiveness is probably one of the hardest things for us as humans to offer. While we have received it as a free blessing and an undeserved gift from God, it is also the biggest challenge of our lives that God asks us to turn around and offer this same forgiveness to others.

CLEARING ⚹ THE ⚹ COBWEBS

While we have received forgiveness as a free blessing and an undeserved gift from God, it is also the biggest challenge of our lives that God asks us to turn around and offer this same forgiveness to others.

Forgiving someone is not saying that what he or she did didn't matter. Forgiving is not a blanket to throw over sin to simply cover it up. Saying, "I forgive you" is not just repartee for "I'm sorry," like replying, "Fine" when someone says, "How are you?" Forgiveness is saying, "You don't owe me anything for what you did." In offering forgiveness to others, we are removing ourselves from the equation and telling them that the matter is between them and God. If we are receiving forgiveness from God, it means that He has promised to clean us up and not remember our sins.

American Red Cross founder Clara Barton was once reminded of an injustice that she had suffered many years before. "Don't you remember?" she was asked. "No," Clara firmly replied. "I distinctly remember forgetting that."

When God does not remember our sins, it is not the same as forgetting, but it is choosing not to bring them up. "As far as the east is from the west, so far has He removed our transgressions from us" (Psalm 103:12). In the same way, we may not forget the things that were done to us, but we can say, "God, I want to show this person the same forgiveness You showed me, no matter what they did."

1. When you were a child, did any of your play buddies ever do anything to you that you didn't want to forgive? Has it gotten harder or easier to forgive as you've grown older?

2. Perhaps elements of your broken past have come about because of other people's wrongdoings. Make a list of excuses you have given yourself at one point of another for withholding forgiveness from these people.

When the Lord forgives us for our sins, He does not say, "No problem. It wasn't really that bad anyway." He knows not only just how bad our sin is, but exactly how sorry we are (or are not). He also knows exactly what it cost Him to be able to offer us this forgiveness. We, who from our earliest childhood days learned to cry out, "It's not fair!" do not often look at what bearing our sins meant for Jesus. It really wasn't fair—Jesus didn't have any sin. He took the punishment for our sins, and the sins of the whole world, and He did it because He knew we could never pay for it ourselves. Accepting the Lord's forgiveness and offering that same forgiveness to others is the key to our restoration.

3. Read Luke's account of Jesus' crucifixion in *Luke 23:26–43*. Write down every insult and cruelty Luke records in the passage.

4. Despite these terrible things, what was Jesus' response to His persecutors?

The Crucifixion is one of the most terrible depictions of cruelty and injustice in the entire Bible, and yet Jesus turned around and offered forgiveness in the midst of His suffering. Not after He had time to process what had happened. Not after He sought counseling or anger therapy. In the hour of His deepest agony, Jesus was modeling exactly what He had come to earth to do—offer forgiveness to people, even to those who don't deserve it.

5. Read the story of the unmerciful servant in *Matthew 18:23–35*. Does this story hit home with you? How many times do we find ourselves playing the part of the unmerciful servant, even though we have accepted God's forgiveness for ourselves?

6. What do you think of the master's response to the unmerciful servant's lack of pity? Does it sound too harsh, or do you think it's about right?

7. What do you think God would say to you right now regarding your level of forgiveness of others?

DIGGING DEEPER

In Matthew 18:35, Jesus says, "My heavenly Father also will do to you [turn us over to the torturers] if each of you, from his heart, does not forgive his brother his trespasses." Why did Jesus say something like this? What does Jesus say in Matthew 18:21-22 about letting the offense go completely when we forgive? What about forgiving ourselves? If we have done something to someone, and they are no longer around to even ask for forgiveness, how do we reconcile those feelings and make things right with God? What if we can't fix it because they don't care or they deny that they did anything wrong? What can we do about those feelings?

PONDER & PRAY

Ask God to show you if you are harboring unforgiving thoughts in your heart toward someone, even if that person is yourself. Take time right now to pray for that person and ask God to help you forgive him or her—and to truly mean it. Pray that the Lord will give you His love toward the people with whom you have difficulties. Pray for someone else whom you know is struggling, and ask that he or she be able to forgive and accept forgiveness.

TRINKETS TO TREASURE

This week's token is a reminder to continually make strides toward forgiveness through prayer. This week, as you ask God to reveal if you are harboring unforgiveness toward someone, make it a point to be intentional about praying over that situation. Set your alarm for a specific time each day—or choose some other form of trigger—and pray for the person you need to forgive at those times. You will be astounded at how God can work!

NOTES & PRAYER REQUESTS

CHAPTER SEVEN

TRUE RECONCILIATION

NOW ALL THINGS ARE OF GOD, WHO HAS RECONCILED US TO HIMSELF THROUGH JESUS CHRIST, AND HAS GIVEN US THE MINISTRY OF RECONCILIATION.

—2 Corinthians 5:18

*A*re you a quick-tempered, argumentative person, or a mellow person who only gets into arguments when someone else picks them? No matter which type of person you are—the type who avoids conflict or the type who revels in it—it is virtually impossible to go through life without entering into a disagreement. And as you know, once you have a disagreement, there are always hurt feelings to soothe, issues to unravel, and relationships to mend.

Reconciling long-term hurts and broken relationships is even more difficult than smoothing over a hot-tempered flare-up. You may have life-long issues that need to be addressed, or estranged relationships that need to be made right. How do you even begin to go about mending problems of this magnitude? In fact, why would you even want to stir up what has been left untouched for so long? Aren't those scars better left unopened?

CLEARING ⚹ THE ⚹ COBWEBS

Why would we want to reopen scars from our past? Because a mended relationship is where true joy and restoration begin!

Cynthia thought so. Her mother had given her away when she was five years old—an act that had caused Cynthia to harbor a lifelong bitterness toward her. Even though she was raised by a loving family, she never understood why her biological mother was unwilling to care for her.

One Saturday after Cynthia had gone off to college, she received a visitor in her dorm room. It was her mother. She had tracked down the daughter she had given away so long ago to ask for her forgiveness. This act of repentance touched Cynthia deeply, and together they began working through all of the hurts and baggage caused by the long-ago decision. It didn't happen overnight, but they both worked hard to develop a relationship—no longer as mother and daughter, but as friends.

Not only did Cynthia offer her forgiveness, but she also chose to try to reconcile their relationship. Thanks to Cynthia's willing spirit, she not only got rid of the bitterness she had carried with her since childhood, but she also discovered more joy than she had ever known before.

1. While it is hard enough to offer forgiveness to those who have wronged you, mending the broken relationship is a whole different ball game. It requires a lot more effort, two-way communication, and time. Have you ever had to reconcile a relationship? What were the circumstances, and what was the outcome?

2. Think back on your past. Do you have any relationships that still need to be reconciled? On a scale of one to ten, one being the lowest and ten being the highest, what is your level of interest in reconciling this relationship? Circle the appropriate number on the scale below.

$$1 - 2 - 3 - 4 - 5 - 6 - 7 - 8 - 9 - 10$$

In 2 Corinthians 5, Paul explains that reconciliation is not a choice; it is a ministry Christ has given each of us. Just as Jesus came to earth to reconcile us to His Father, so should we reconcile ourselves to our brothers and sisters in Christ.

3. Read 2 Corinthians 5:11–21. Verse 19 gives us the definition of reconciliation (read the NIV translation for a clearer description). When Christ reconciles us to God, what is He doing? In return, if we are to be like Christ, what should we do? What would this look like in your life?

4. The first step to true reconciliation is to be reconciled to God. We are then to be His ambassadors as we spread the news of reconciliation to others. Do you spread the news about what Christ has done for you regularly? What holds you back from doing so?

While God has made it clear that He wishes for us to be reconciled to Him and to our brothers and sisters in Christ, how do we do this practically? Jesus knew that reconciliation does not come naturally to us sinful humans, so He gave us a model in His Word of what true reconciliation looks like.

5. Read Matthew 18:15–20. Jesus gave us a process we should go through with people who have wronged us. List the steps below.

6. Have you ever dealt with a problem between you and someone else in a different manner than Jesus described? How did you deal with it? What was the outcome?

7. Read Ephesians 4:25–32. How does this passage say we must speak to our neighbor? What must we be careful not to do when we are angry?

8. What are ways in which you can get rid of all "bitterness, wrath, anger, clamor, and evil speech"? List a few below.

By giving us these guidelines, I don't believe Jesus meant to be legalistic. He did, however, mean to give us an example of an appropriate way to deal with those who are wrong. He knows that, if left up to our own manner of doing things, we would very likely cause more damage than good. Only when we adopt the nature of Christ and deal with people as Christ dealt with us are we able to not only offer forgiveness but also work toward reconciliation. And a mended relationship is where true joy and restoration begin!

DIGGING DEEPER

Before we approach our brothers or sisters about something they have done, we must take an honest evaluation of our own lives. In Luke 6:42, Jesus said, "How can you say to your brother, 'Brother, let me remove the speck that is in your eye,' when you yourself do not see the plank that is in your own eye? Hypocrite! First remove the plank from your own eye, and then you will see clearly to remove the speck that is in your brother's eye." Do not accuse your brother of something of which you yourself may be guilty. When you look at your life honestly, do you have anything about which you need to come clean before you approach someone else about his or her wrongdoing?

PONDER & PRAY

Spend some time asking God to point out any situation that you need to reconcile. Pray that God would give you wisdom in how to approach the person, that he or she would have a mollified heart, and that the person would listen to what you have to say. Pray that you would have a spirit of humility—not anger—when you approach him or her. Pray also that not only would you forgive that person, but also that Christ would restore your heart despite the wrongdoing.

TRINKETS TO TREASURE

This week's token is a reminder that some hurts between people are deeper and more serious than others. Much like a broken bone that must be set and bandaged, these types of wounds will require more time for healing to occur. However, the first step is the same. No matter what our situation is or the nature of the hurt, we need to take one small step right now to begin the process of mending the broken relationship. So, as you think about this, what is that one small step you will take this week?

Notes & Prayer Requests

CHAPTER EIGHT

Even When It's Not Fair

What does the Lord require of you but to do justly, to love mercy, and to walk humbly with your God?

—Micah 6:8

W e tend to have a highly developed sense of justice as children. It's "not fair" that the kid next to us got a bigger piece of birthday cake. The first response to our competitor beating us in tag is, "But he cheated!" We sense that it is somehow not okay that a bully should be able to take our lunch money from us when he already has his own.

From an early age, we learn that life is not exactly fair. This knowledge only intensifies as we mature, and the evidence we can cite becomes more serious. A football player on our college team is killed in a random drive-by shooting. Our husband's business partner embezzles funds and leaves him—and our family—bankrupt. A drunk driver takes the life of our friend as she is coming home from choir practice.

It's hard to believe how these seemingly random occurrences could have been allowed to happen by a benevolent God. And when it touches

Clearing ↗ the ↖ Cobwebs

As much as we may want to wallow in our own suffering, the truth is that everyone goes through it. Suffering is as old as sin itself.

our lives, we ask, "Why did this happen to us, Lord?" Our hearts cry out for justice, even if there is none to be found.

We all have our stories of suffering. The Lord blessed my husband and me with six children—four to raise and two to send back to heaven as babies. They were both born with certain nonhereditary birth defects, lived short and precious lives, and brought their parents to Jesus. When our third baby, the second to die, had gone on to be with the Lord, I sat in the predawn, rocking our grieving three-year-old. Beside us was the empty basket, with a rumpled blanket and dimpled sheets where a living child had rested the day before.

My first daughter, Lizzie, nestled on my shoulder as we talked about her lost sister, how much we loved her, and that she was safe and well in the arms of Jesus. And I remembered all the ways that the Lord had been faithful to us during her short life. Not one time did I cry out and He not answer. Even when my baby dies, Jesus is enough, I remember thinking. And then, If even once I can tell that to someone else, it will have been worth it.

1. What is the most "unfair" occurrence that you have witnessed or had happen to you? Perhaps you only saw it on a news report, or maybe you were actually the victim. What were the circumstances, and what were the results?

2. Did anything good come out of this terrible situation?

As much as we may want to wallow in our own suffering, the truth is that everyone goes through it. Suffering is as old as sin itself. In fact, the Old Testament dedicates an entire book to the suffering of a righteous man.

3. Read Job 1:1–22. What does the very first verse of this chapter tell us about Job? In your opinion, why do you think God would let all of these things happen to someone who had served Him so faithfully?

4. List everything that Satan did to Job in this chapter. Compare Job's response with what your response would have been under the same circumstances.

Despite his immense suffering, Job never cried out against God. He questioned God. He asked for God's mercy. But he remained a faithful servant through it all.

Other servants have given up their very lives to remain faithful. After Jesus' death, Rome became a dangerous place for Christians to voice their faith. In the face of horrific and unjust persecution, countless saints gave up their lives to follow Jesus. Hebrews 11 says of these saints:

> Others were tortured, not accepting deliverance, that they might obtain a better resurrection. Still others had trial of mockings and scourgings, yes, and of chains and imprisonment. They were stoned, they were sawn in two, were tempted, were slain with the sword. They wandered about in sheepskins and goatskins, being destitute, afflicted, tormented—of whom the world was not worthy. They wandered in deserts and mountains, in dens and caves of the earth. And all these, having obtained a good testimony through faith, did not receive the promise, God having provided something better for us, that they should not be made perfect apart from us. (Hebrews 11:35–40)

5. These saints endured sufferings that many of us can only imagine— and we likely don't want to imagine! Consider where you are in your walk with Christ. At this point, do you think you would have been able to do the same? Why or why not?

6. Take a look at verse 39. Even though these saints endured such hardships, they still did not receive what was promised them by God! How does this change your perspective regarding the timing you may expect from God?

7. What does Jesus say in Matthew 6:19–20 about where we should place our values? How does this relate to how we should look at life when unfair things happen to us?

Doesn't it help to realize that others besides yourself have suffered? And perhaps it was even part of God's plan? Jochabed lost her baby boy at about three months when he was taken away to be raised by foreigners who despised Jochabed's people. Her son was Moses. Despite his upbringing, Moses grew to be a humble man, a faithful servant of the living God.

Mary watched her Son die on the cross. Did she remember the words of old Simeon when she carried the baby Jesus to the temple? "Yes, a sword will pierce through your own soul also" (Luke 2:35). Jesus, the Son of God, died the death of a felon, and rescued the whole world. If our God can make something so good come from something so bad, can He not also bring good out of our own sufferings?

That is one of the reasons we suffer. We can be the arms of Jesus to others, and tell them that He will never let them down, and they believe us because we have lived it.

DIGGING DEEPER

Read Micah 6:8, the verse quoted at the opening of this lesson. This verse certainly simplifies things for us, doesn't it? All God requires of us is to walk humbly with Him. Through the storms, through the deserts, through the times of plenty, He will be our guide. How does this concept make you look at suffering differently?

PONDER & PRAY

Spend some time in prayer telling the Lord how you feel about everything you have gone through. Be completely honest with Him; He can handle it. Then ask God to help you find the silver lining in your suffering. If you've already found the silver lining, thank Him for His provision and wisdom. Even try thanking Him for the suffering. After all, suffering is an opportunity to deepen your relationship with Him.

TRINKETS TO TREASURE

"When life gives you lemons, make lemonade!" How many times have we heard people tell us that when we're going through a rough time? We may have appreciated their kind remarks or we may have wanted to slap them, but that doesn't lessen the truth of the statement: good things can come from bad. This week's token is a reminder of that fact. You may even want to make some fresh-squeezed lemonade this week (or buy it at the store and pretend it's fresh squeezed!). As you drink it, you can think of all the sour, seemingly unredeemable lemons it took to create such a sweet beverage. Then you can think of how you can "add a little sugar" to a sour situation in your own life.

NOTES & PRAYER REQUESTS

CHAPTER NINE

The Power of Joy

But the fruit of the Spirit is love, joy, peace, longsuffering, kindness, goodness, faithfulness, gentleness, self-control.

—Galatians 5:22–23

What exactly is joy? You hear preachers and Sunday school teachers talk about it. You've read about it in the Bible. But doesn't it sound more like a myth than something that could actually be true—kind of like the Easter Bunny or the Tooth Fairy? After all, how could this magical "feel-good" sentiment follow you around from circumstance to circumstance, no matter what it is you're going through? We've each been through some pretty bad things, and we weren't always feeling so good about them! This joy concept seems impossible, right?

Well, I hate to break it to you, but it is impossible . . . on our own. On our own, there is no way we will ever be content when our husband leaves us or be able to say "I am okay" when we watch our mother lose her long battle against cancer. On our own, our broken past will always be just that—broken, unrestored, and incredibly painful.

CLEARING ✄ THE ⤙ COBWEBS

The truth is, if we can learn how to apply joy liberally in our lives, that is how we will truly be set free.

Before you start wailing in despair, however, let me tell you the other side of the coin. God did not create us to be on our own! He wants us to walk with Him, and "in [His] presence is fullness of joy" (Psalm 16:11). There's that joy word again, and apparently it can be found in God's presence. But how will it help us?

Joy—a sense of well-being that surpasses circumstances. If you could bottle it, it would be the best thing since anti-aging cream. It would fly off store shelves because it's what everyone wants but doesn't know how to get. Imagine being able to say, "Everything is right with the world because I know God is in control," no matter what happens to you! That is joy. And what is the result of joy? Healing from brokenness. If we can learn how to apply joy liberally in our lives, that is how we will truly be set free.

Though joy cannot be found in a bottle or a tube, it can be found in Christ. And it is the secret to complete restoration. Joy gives us the ability to rise above our past, be content in our present, and look forward to our future.

1. If you could buy your idea of the perfect spiritual "miracle cream," what would it do for you? Would it erase your memory of a certain time, help you treat others better, make you feel loved?

2. Can you remember a time when joy has helped you rise above something that happened to you? Explain.

Thankfully, through Christ we have complete and unrestricted access to the "miracle cream" of joy. In Galatians, Paul tells us that joy is one of the fruits of the Holy Spirit, meaning that—like a tree that bears fruit as it matures—joy is one of the fruits we will bear as we grow in our relationship with Jesus.

3. Read Galatians 5:16–26. According to this passage, there are two types of fruit—desires of the evil nature and fruits of the Spirit. List each type of fruit in the two different columns below. What is the difference between these two types of fruit?

Desires of the Evil Nature   Fruits of the Spirit

_____   _____

_____   _____

_____   _____

_____   _____

_____   _____

_____   _____

_____   _____

_____   _____

_____   _____

_____   _____

_____   _____

4. Now that we know what the good fruits are, how do we begin bearing them? What does John 15:1–11 say about this?

5. What does it mean to abide, or remain, in Christ? On a scale of one to ten, one being the lowest and ten the highest, how well do you think you are abiding in Christ at this moment in your life? Explain.

$$1 - 2 - 3 - 4 - 5 - 6 - 7 - 8 - 9 - 10$$

6. In verse 11, Jesus tells us that He has told us these things so His joy will be in us and our joy will be full. What do you make of this statement?

The key to a life full of joy is remaining in God's love. Within God's love, we are able to take a heavenly perspective on our circumstances, realizing that there is more to life than meets the eye. Fanny Crosby, for example, was blind from early childhood. Despite her affliction, she wrote hundreds of hymns that never whisper of her burdens. Her husband was blind too. There is a story of someone stopping in to visit them one day, and finding the two of them laughing and talking together, having a good time with their music. They were both blind, the wallpaper was coming down in their living room, their surroundings were dingy, but the joy in their lives superseded their circumstances.

Joy is a choice. Fanny Crosby chose to view her circumstances through a heavenly lens and find joy in everything. As James says, "Count it all joy."

7. Read James 1:2. The word count indicates that we must make the active choice to find joy in our circumstances. How easy would it be for you to count it all joy? Are you practiced at choosing joy, or are you used to focusing on the negative? In your opinion, which is the better way to live?

Without Christ, our past is destined to become our future. We will continue to indulge in our sinful nature, reaping contentions, jealousies, selfish ambitions, and wrath—all hurtful and self-destructive characteristics. But by remaining in Christ, we no longer have to look at life in the same way. We will bear fruits of joy, peace, and love—the building blocks of a restored past and a hopeful future.

DIGGING DEEPER

Read Philippians 4:4–7. Paul wrote the book of Philippians when he was in prison, yet he had a lot to say about joy. What does this tell you about the source of joy? What does it mean to rejoice in the Lord always? How can you honestly rejoice in the Lord when your life is full of sorrow or confusion? How does choosing to rejoice in the Lord indicate that you are looking at your circumstances from a heavenly perspective?

PONDER & PRAY

Spend some time thinking about which fruits of the Spirit you would like to see grow in your life, and then pray for this growth. Praise the Lord for the good things that He has done, and like Paul, rejoice! Pray that you will learn how to count it all joy, and that you would discover what true joy looks like.

TRINKETS TO TREASURE

When runners train for a race, they use a stopwatch to "count" the time it took for them to reach the finish line. In this way, they can keep track of how their pain and effort during training is helping them to achieve a better time. This week's token is a stopwatch to remind us of this same truth in life. It is by looking back and seeing what we have come through that we will be able to appreciate where we are in the present. So, this week, write down several bad things that have happened to you or someone you know. Once you have recorded these, write down a way that you can "count" each item as joy. Try to make this a regular practice in your life so you can develop a habit of looking at things joyfully.

Notes & Prayer Requests

CHAPTER TEN

JOY IN SUFFERING

FOR HIS ANGER IS BUT FOR A MOMENT, HIS FAVOR
IS FOR LIFE; WEEPING MAY ENDURE FOR A NIGHT,
BUT JOY COMES IN THE MORNING.

—Psalm 30:5

No one enjoys a toothache or a broken foot. We don't say, "Whoopee! The kids all have chicken pox!" Throwing up with stomach flu is not an opportunity to celebrate. Yet we can all appreciate the philosophy that says, "The kids are sick, but I'm not going to complain. We'll read lots of stories and put on some good music and get through it." Isn't it much easier to take care of someone who is a cheerful invalid than a complainer?

Suffering is a part of life, and some times are more painful than others. As we seek healing from brokenness, we have to be honest about the pain. But the good news is that pain is not the sole result of suffering! As Romans 5:3–4 tells us, we should rejoice in tribulations, for "tribulation produces perseverance; and perseverance, character; and character, hope." But how do we make the leap from suffering to hope and rejoicing?

On a January day many years ago our little girl, Rose, was born with none of her inner lung

CLEARING THE COBWEBS

The truth is, suffering and joy can go hand in hand because suffering is not the end of the story. Joy is the end of the story.

sacs closed. She died before we had a chance to get to know her. "Don't worry," the doctor said, "there is only one chance in ten thousand that it could ever happen again." That was comforting, but there was still no little girl to take home with us.

The next day a friend came bursting in the door, eager to see the new baby. I had to tell her that the baby was dead. There she was, with her two little ones and their crayon drawings that they had made for my new child. I couldn't help but think, *Would I ever have little children too?*

Letters came from friends far away. Women my grandmother's age shared their losses. I had no idea that some of them had buried children, too, and it touched my heart and drew me close to them. A friend and neighbor from my childhood shared some deep spiritual wisdom. She told me that when Bradley, her son, had died in a car accident the year before, the only thing that took away that empty gnawing feeling in her stomach was when she began to praise the Lord for taking Bradley home. She said that she knew that God loved him, and it was her job to trust God with his death as well as she had tried to with his life. If I could begin to praise the Lord for Rose's death, she thought I would find healing.

I thought it was about the stupidest thing I had ever heard. I wasn't blaming God, but I didn't think that thanking Him for the death of my baby would help anything, either. Because this woman was an old family friend, though, I decided to try her advice.

"I praise You, Lord, that Rose died," I said. "I don't mean it, but I am saying it." I was taking a shower, and it was a good time to think and pray as the hot water washed over me. *Why could it be good for Rose to die?* I wondered. Some glimmering of the bigness and goodness of God began to dawn on me. "I praise You, Lord, that You took Rose to heaven." That time I meant it a little more. The more I thought about praising the Lord for taking our little baby, the more I began to think about who He really is. I found that He does indeed give "beauty for ashes, the oil of joy for mourning" (Isaiah 61:3).

If we can honestly say that "knowing God is more important than anything" when we have experienced pain and loss, "I don't hate You" when there is every earthly reason to hate, and "I trust You with the future" when the future has suddenly gone blank, our words are far more meaningful than if said when all is right with the world. In times when some people sink into bitterness and despair, others rise above to be good soldiers for Jesus. The question to ask ourselves is, *Do I want to give this to Jesus to use for His glory?*

We don't choose many of the things that come our way. Some we would avoid at all cost if we could. Yet there is one thread through all of the stories of people who have lived as shining Christians in the direst circumstances. They can say, "I never want to do that again, but I would not change those dreadful days because of the things I learned about my Lord."

Suffering and joy can go hand in hand because suffering is not the end of the story. Joy is the end of the story. If the suffering we have endured gives us the credentials to be believed when we tell others about Jesus, then that suffering turns into a jewel for the King.

1. Have you ever praised God for a trial that you have endured? Did you praise Him immediately or did it take a while for you to be able to get to that point?

One reason God allows us to endure trials is to be able to identify with others who have suffered. Horatio Spafford wrote "It Is Well with My Soul" after his children had been drowned in a shipwreck. Though he had gone through something terrible, the fruit of his suffering has brought comfort to countless people who have heard this song.

2. Have you ever been able to use your trial to help someone who is going through the same thing? Explain.

3. Read Hebrews 2:18. How does it make you feel knowing that Christ can help us in our suffering because He went through everything we have and will go through? How is this a model for the way we should react to others?

In the song "It Is Well with My Soul," Horatio did not say, "I'm so happy because of everything I'm going through! All of this suffering is so much fun!" No, he wasn't able to say that. But he could say, "Whatever my lot, Thou has taught me to say, it is well, it is well, with my soul."

4. What is the difference between saying "I'm so happy," and "It is well with my soul"?

5. Read 1 Peter 4:12–16. Why should we not be surprised when we experience trials? Why should we consider them to be blessings?

6. In what ways is this passage seemingly contradictory? What other examples of this "opposite thinking" can you find in the Bible? (To get started, check out the Sermon on the Mount in Matthew 5:1–11.)

By looking at life from a heavenly point of view, we are able to gain a new perspective on our tribulations. God's plans and timing are not our plans and timing—as much as we wish they were—but He does promise to give us joy, no matter what curveball is thrown at us!

7. In the last chapter we read James 1:2–3 and talked about joy being a choice. Can you count it all joy, even when you endure trials? Have you ever tried to do this? What happened?

8. Psalm 30:5 promises that "weeping may endure for a night, but joy comes in the morning." How does this promise give you hope? Have you ever experienced the results of this promise?

DIGGING DEEPER

What parts of your broken past would you label as "fiery trials"? What have you learned about God from these times? Have you been able to pass these truths on to others? It is not always easy to sort out the jewels from the pebbles as we sift through painful times in our lives. Our perspective might change as we grow in the Lord. But if we give our lives to Jesus—the past as well as the future—He can show us how the very things that seem the worst times in our lives are, when they are put in His hands, credentials to speak the truth about salvation, forgiveness, and the love of Christ.

PONDER & PRAY

In Colossians 1:9–12, Paul writes, "For this reason we also, since the day we heard it, do not cease to pray for you, and to ask that you may be filled with the knowledge of His will in all wisdom and spiritual understanding; that you may walk worthy of the Lord, fully pleasing Him, being fruitful in every good work and increasing in the knowledge of God; strengthened with all might, according to His glorious power, for all patience and long-suffering with joy; giving thanks to the Father who has qualified us to be partakers of the inheritance of the saints in the light."

Pray this prayer for your family, your small group, and/or your friends. Go over it again in the week ahead, praying for yourself and those around you.

TRINKETS TO TREASURE

This week's token is a dove to remind us of the peace that Jesus brings in the midst of even the worst times of suffering. As you think of this image, sometime this week look up the lyrics online to the song, "It Is Well with My Soul." Keep in mind what the songwriter was going through as he wrote these lyrics. Take a moment to remember how you feel after reading them. Do you identify with the words? Does the message give you hope? Why or why not?

NOTES & PRAYER REQUESTS

CHAPTER ELEVEN

JOYFUL FOR OTHERS

FOR WE ARE HIS WORKMANSHIP, CREATED IN CHRIST JESUS FOR GOOD WORKS, WHICH GOD PREPARED BEFOREHAND THAT WE SHOULD WALK IN THEM.

—Ephesians 2:10

Each one of us is unique in form and feature, time and space, gifts and talents. We have been born into a family with certain traits, heritages, and walks of life. We have been given many unique experiences, some edifying and others destructive. Whether we like it or not, these experiences compose our past—good or bad—and have created who we are today.

Coming out of your broken past, it may have seemed impossible that you would ever experience joy again. And it may have seemed more impossible still that you would ever be able to share joy with others. But the truth is, in order to receive joy in the first place, we must focus on others instead of ourselves.

My friend Diane was diagnosed with multiple sclerosis. During the sickness, she learned that she would never be able to be happy if she focused on herself and her circumstances. "I used to pray, 'Heal me, heal me,'" she confided, talking in the

CLEARING 𐌀 THE 𐌊 COBWEBS

The truth is, in order to receive joy in the first place, we must focus on others instead of ourselves.

81

halting manner that was now normal for her. "But He didn't do that. So I prayed, 'Take me, take me,' and He didn't do that, either. Finally I prayed, 'Use me.' And He has shown me how to pray."

Those of us who were her friends and family were the beneficiaries. "I pray for you every day," she told me. God bless her, I needed those prayers.

Diane didn't come to this position quickly. She had weeks of struggles, followed by times of more comfort, and then more struggles. It was no easier for her to lay down the reins of her life than it would be for any of the rest of us. Her children were young, she had a good husband, and the usual responsibilities and activities of any mother involved in church and community life. She didn't pray because she had nothing else to do. She prayed because she had come to understand that it was the most important thing she could do, and the Lord had put her in the position where she had time to do it. Diane said that she would never trade her health for the things that she now knows about the Lord.

The things that we learn as we deal with our own brokenness are tools that we can most readily use to relate to others who are as joyless as we once were. Just as God comforts us with His love, focusing on helping others is the easiest way to forget about our own problems and share joy with those in need.

We know from the New Testament accounts that Paul was comforted when others saw his physical needs and met them. Paul describes the Philippian church's generosity as a "sweet smelling aroma" to him. Though he suffered trials and want without complaining, when the Philippians took the time to care for him he felt extremely blessed. He told them, "Indeed I have all and abound. I am full, having received from Epaphroditus the things sent from you, a sweet-smelling aroma, an acceptable sacrifice, well pleasing to God" (Philippians 4:18).

When we have the fruit of love to give to others, it is sweet to the Lord, and we are on the path to true joy and freedom.

1. Describe a time when you did something good for someone in need. Did helping others make it easier for you to get your mind off your own problems? Did it give you joy?

2. What could God be calling you to do right now? Take a quick evaluation of your present circumstances, and in the space below jot down a few possibilities that come to mind.

God did not have to create humans. He could have existed alone in the universe, without the unavoidable pain He knew would result from giving humans the choice between good and evil. But even knowing everything in advance—the Fall of humanity, the generations of people who would reject Him, and the death of His Son for our atonement—God chose to endure the pain so He could also experience the love we would give Him. In the same way, though we have been hurt by others, the joy we receive by helping those around us is infinitely greater than the security of hiding behind our pain.

3. When we think of doing something good, we want it to be noble, but not all that difficult. When we read Luke 6:27–36, however, we receive a different perspective. Have you ever chosen to help someone, even if it didn't seem to be in your best interest?

4. How does this passage ask you to be the "bigger person"? How is it a sign of spiritual maturity when you are able to do as Jesus tells you to in this passage?

Every life experience you have had defines who you are. God knew exactly what you would go through when He allowed you to be born into this world, and because of these things, you have been equipped to help others in a way that no one else can.

5. What does Psalm 139:15–16 tell us about how much God knew of our future before we were even born?

6. Write out Romans 8:28 in the space below. After reading this verse, do you believe God can coordinate your past to put you in a unique position to help people in your present? Explain.

7. Second Corinthians 1:3–11 is a great passage on comfort. Rephrase verse four in your own words. How does this verse shed new light on how you can relate to others?

DIGGING DEEPER

Ephesians 2:10, the verse quoted at the beginning of the chapter, tells us that God has prepared good works for us to do. Do you think you have been identifying these good works and doing them? If not, what has been holding you back? If so, how does it feel to focus on others instead of yourself? Has it increased your joy?

PONDER & PRAY

Pray that God would continue to reveal the works He has planned for you. Pray that you would be selfless enough to help others, even if it's difficult. Pray that God would help you use the pain you have gone through to bring joy to others, and in return, yourself.

TRINKETS TO TREASURE

This week's token will remind you of the opportunities that abound to help the needy in your world. This could be volunteering for a position in your church, or serving in a community soup kitchen, or even taking an overseas missions trip. No matter what you choose to do, keep in mind that God calls each of us to reach out to others and share our joy with those in need.

NOTES & PRAYER REQUESTS

CHAPTER TWELVE

ONWARD TOWARD THE GOAL

I HAVE FOUGHT THE GOOD FIGHT, I HAVE FINISHED THE RACE,
I HAVE KEPT THE FAITH. FINALLY, THERE IS LAID UP FOR ME
THE CROWN OF RIGHTEOUSNESS, WHICH THE LORD, THE
RIGHTEOUS JUDGE, WILL GIVE TO ME ON THAT DAY, AND NOT
TO ME ONLY BUT ALSO TO ALL WHO HAVE LOVED APPEARING.

—2 Timothy 4:7–8

Back in the early '60s, when I was in junior high and small country schools had no sports programs for girls, a group of us began to agitate for a girl's track team. Our physical education teacher thought he would discourage us and took us out to run on the boys' cross-country training trail. We knew we were being tested, but we were determined not to give up. For the first time I experienced that phenomena of "getting your second wind," which I had only read about in books. At the point when I thought my aching lungs would take no more, there was a sense of release and my body settled into the rhythm of running. We finished the course as a group, rather smug and very cheerful. Despite our best efforts, we still weren't allowed to have a girls' track team, but we learned the importance of finishing the race we began.

CLEARING ⋊ THE ⋉ COBWEBS

Our job is to forget that which is past and press on toward the goal. There is not one thing on earth we can do that is more important than knowing and loving Jesus as our Lord and Savior, and this should always be our primary focus.

The quest for helaing from a broken past may be a long one—and one that won't completely end until we cross the finish line and enter heaven. Suffering is a regular part of the race, but we have also learned that there will be joy throughout the course. What's important is continuously getting our second wind and running, running, running!

Paul had a lot in his past to get over. For starters, he was with the men who stoned Stephen to death because he was a Christian. Paul is described as "breathing out murderous threats" against the believers, and he was eager to catch and imprison those who were worshiping Jesus. Besides persecuting Christians, he was also very proud of his education and spotless Jewish ancestry.

When he was stopped en route to Damascus, his whole life changed overnight. But even after years of being one of the greatest missionaries the world has ever seen, Paul still did not consider that he had attained what he was striving for in being like Jesus. But he did know one thing: "Forgetting those things which are behind and reaching forward to those things which are ahead, I press toward the goal for the prize of the upward call of God in Christ Jesus" (Philippians 3:13–14).

Like Paul, our job is to forget that which is past and press on toward the goal. There is not one thing on earth we can do that is more important than knowing and loving Jesus as our Lord and Savior, and this should always be our primary focus.

1. Have you ever had to run or walk a great distance? Did you get tired out and want to give up? How did you press through it?

2. As you have been working through this study, have you gotten better at "forgetting those things which are behind"? Explain where you were when you began the study and where you are now.

3. Do you feel as if you have reached the "point of perfection" in your quest to be like Jesus? Do you have any motivating factors that push you onward, or do you get burnt out and discouraged easily? Give examples of these motivating factors, if you have them.

Hebrews 12 is a splendid chapter that gives us great encouragement, especially in the first two verses:

> Therefore we also, since we are surrounded by so great a cloud of witnesses, let us lay aside every weight, and the sin which so easily ensnares us, and let us run with endurance the race that is set before us, looking unto Jesus, the author and finisher of our faith, who for the joy that was set before Him endured the cross, despising the shame, and has sat down at the right hand of the throne of God." (Hebrews 12:1–2)

Not only is this an inspiring passage that makes me want to strap on a pair of running shoes and get some road under my feet, but it also tells us we have a "great cloud of witnesses" watching our progress! And these aren't just any witnesses—they are the saints who lived before us, who also endured great difficulties, just like us. Imagine—the greats, like Abraham, Peter, Job, and John, all care about our journey and are cheering us on!

4. When you think of all the saints who want you to succeed in your race, do you feel inspired? Is there anyone in particular whom you can picture looking down at you?

5. If the saints were to provide a commentary of your progress, what would they say about how you are running your race?

6. This "great cloud of witnesses" can also be interpreted as our peers—both fellow Christians and those who do not know Jesus—watching us as we live our lives. Are you following the example of those who have gone before you? Are you setting a good example for those who are coming behind you? What would your peers say about the legacy you are leaving?

7. Is there a particular weight or sin that you have had trouble laying aside? How has this impeded your progress? How would your life be different if you could get rid of this ensnaring sin once and for all?

8. Take a few minutes to think back over your progress throughout this study, and write a brief synopsis in the space below. What was the most important lesson you learned? What was the hardest truth you had to face? Are you ready to continue running the race to the finish line?

DIGGING DEEPER

Read James 1:12. What does this verse say we will receive at the end of the race? What does a crown of life mean? Why is this the most motivating factor that we could have to help spur us on? Though the race is long and the end may not seem to be in sight, just remember that we can run with joy, for we have a crown of life awaiting us at the finish line!

PONDER & PRAY

Pray that God would continue to give you joy, and that it might be displayed in your life for the world to see. Pray for those whom you have forgiven, that God would be with them, changing their lives day by day. Pray for your future, that you would continue to walk in the path of righteousness. Pray for steadfastness, and that God would give you the motivation to finish the race.

TRINKETS TO TREASURE

This week's token will remind you that our journey through life is often like running a race. As Paul says, we "press toward the goal for the prize of the upward call of God" (Phillipians 3:14). To this end, think about walking or running a literal race this week. Research the 5Ks (3 miles), 10Ks (6 miles), or even half marathons (13.1 miles) in your community. Many of these races benefit charities and are for good causes. More important, such an activity will help you truly understand the biblical reference of how we should press on in life.

NOTES & PRAYER REQUESTS

Shall We Review?

Every chapter has added a new trinket to your treasure trove of memories. Let's remind ourselves of the lessons they hold for us!

1. Journal

Be sure to start keeping a record of your progress each week. After each lesson, write a few sentences to help you remember what you've learned and how far you've come.

2. Family Portrait

All believers in Christ have been adopted into God's family. Consider being a blessing to a child who may not have been fortunate enough to have the love of a family

3. Mirror

It's important to take an honest "look in the mirror" from time to time to see if there are any areas in which we still feel entrapped by our past sins.

4. List

This list will serve as a reminder of all the times God has given us rest and provision in the midst of our problems. We can be encouraged when we are reminded of all the ways God has provided for us in the past.

5. Letter

We need to be continually reaching out to others with forgiveness. This week's token reminds us to reach to someone whom we may have formerly blamed for our problems.

6. Alarm Clock

We need reminders throughout our day to be intentional about praying over those situations in which we have harbored unforgiveness toward someone.

7. Bandage

Some hurts between people are more serious than others and make take years to heal. We need to take small steps to begin the process of healing.

8. Pitcher of Lemonade

It's often tough to accept but nonetheless true that good things can come from made. This week's token will remind us that when life gives us lemons, we can choose to make lemonade!

9. Stopwatch

Runners keep track of their time during a race to see how their pain and effort is paying off over time. We can likewise learn to "count" the good things that have come out of difficult or painful circumstances in the past.

10. Dove

The symbol of the dove reminds us of peace. The week, we need to remember that Jesus brings us His peace and joy even in the midst of difficult times of suffering.

11. Globe

Opportunities abound in our world today to help those in need. God calls each of us to reach out to others and share the joy that He has given to us.

12. Runner

Our journey through life is often like running a race. As we press on in faithfully serving Christ, we can be confident in knowing we will one day receive our eternal reward.

LEADER'S GUIDE

Chapter 1: A Broken World

Focus: The truth is, we live in a broken world, and we are all products of its depravity. Each and every one of us has not only dealt with the repercussions of people's bad actions, but if we look inward at ourselves, we can see that it's not always other people who are to blame.

1. Answers may vary. This is an opportunity for your group to begin building trust with one another by sharing stories of celebrities, people in the news, or even friends (although you might remind them to withhold names of those others in the group might know) whom they have seen make bad choices because of things that have happened in their past.

2. Keep in mind that each of your group members comes from a different past with varying degrees of brokenness. This could be the beginning of a very difficult journey for one woman, while another woman has had an uneventful past but still seeks a community of God-fearing women to keep her on the right path. Be sensitive to all levels of brokenness, and never push someone to share something they don't want to. Assure all of the women that everyone is a sinner, and no one is better than anyone else.

3. Jesus knew the truth about the Samaritan woman. He told her that she was living with a man who was not her husband and that she had had five husbands before him. Despite this shameful fact, Jesus still chose to speak to her, and viewed her as a life worth redeeming. This shows us that we can hide nothing from Jesus, for He knows each and every one of our secrets. If you feel that your group is not ready to share, allow the second part of the question to be rhetorical and just have the women think about things that Jesus knows about them.

4. The Scriptures tell us that the woman left her waterpot, went into the city, and called others to come hear Jesus' words. She was impressed by His ability to tell her everything she ever did, to the extent that, despite her low standing in the community, she faced ridicule and scorn to convince others that Jesus was the Messiah.

5. It may help to make a chart like the one below:

SPIRITUAL	LITERAL
Jesus told the woman that He could give her living water.	She asked how He could give her living water if He had no bucket from which to draw from the well.
Jesus told the woman she would never thirst again.	She wanted this living water so she would not have to keep coming to the well to draw water.
Jesus answered that a time would come when they would worship in spirit and truth, and the physical location would not matter.	She told Jesus that the Samaritans and the Jews must worship in a physical location.

6. Answers may vary, but is easy to be blinded by circumstances instead of looking at the good things God wants to show us. For example, if a close relative died, it is so easy to be caught up in our grief that we do not see others joining together to comfort us. Push people to come up with examples.

7. Answers may vary. This is an opportunity for people to express their perceptions of God and what they believe He can do.

8. Jeremiah 29:11 tells us, "'For I know the plans I have for you,' declares the Lord, 'plans to prosper you and not to harm you, plans to give you hope and a future'" (NIV). These are words of great comfort, for they assure us that God has wonderful plans for each of us, even if we can't see them at the moment. Assure the women in your group that no matter what they have been through, God can still bring good out of evil.

Chapter 2: Adopted by God

Focus: The truth is that He loves each one of us as a person, no matter what we have done or what has happened to us. He made you, He willingly paid for you through Jesus' death, and He wants to see your face at our family reunion in heaven along with the rest of His adopted children.

1. Answers may vary depending on experiences. People could have had a wonderful experience with adoption or it could have been horrible if they were not placed in a loving family. Good experiences, however, probably resulted in love, good relationships, and feelings of gratitude toward those who adopted them. God wants each of us to be adopted by Him so He can love and care for us, and help restore our sinful pasts.

2. This is a sensitive question meant to allow women to express their stories of salvation. If you sense that a member of your group has not been saved, do not pressure her to announce this to the group if she doesn't want to. Just commit to praying for her and hope that by the end of the study she will feel the need for God in her life.

3. Paul is saying that God has planned in advance that each and every one of us would be adopted by Him! Not only that, but it is through His "pleasure" and His "will" that this was made possible. This is a very encouraging verse, because no matter what our pasts were like, God still chose each and every one of us to be His adopted children.

4. Chose is a very active word that indicates intention. God intentionally went out of His way to choose us as His own.

5. Not only did God choose each and every one of us, but He did so before the world began! Make this point by asking the women how far in advance they plan things. You may have women who buy Christmas gifts in July, or women who plan a dinner party the day of the event. But people cannot truthfully claim that they have ever planned anything before the world began, or even at the beginning of their lives.

6. Sons (and daughters!) of God are led by the Spirit of God. This means that they make choices that God would be pleased with—kind of a WWJD reminder.

7. Answers may differ for each person, but the gist of the answer is that no one needs to fear anything from their past because we have been set free by God. We don't need to fear the repercussions of bad decisions we've made because God is there to help us deal with them. We don't need to fear people who have harmed or scared us in the past, either. We are free to live!

Chapter 3: Free Indeed

Focus: The truth is that we may have one sin acting as the biggest obstacle to freedom, the simplest sin we don't even notice—thinking that our past is too overwhelming for God to do anything about.

1. Answers could include the following emotions: shame from what she had done, fear for her life, hostility toward her accusers, anger at herself and those around her, incredulity at what was happening to her, even terror at what was going to happen next. Guide the women through thinking about each of these answers, and as they disclose if they have ever felt this way.

2. There is no right answer to this question; it is all speculation. But Jesus could have wanted to remove Himself from the self-righteous accusers by taking a step back; He could have been writing the sins of the people accusing the woman in the dirt in order to remind them of their own transgressions; He could have wanted to maintain a passive demeanor in order to diffuse the volatile situation. There are many possibilities. Explore them with the group.

3. The Pharisees were trying to trap Jesus into saying that the adulterous woman should not be stoned, which would be directly in contrast with what the Law said. So instead of answering directly, Jesus threw the burden on the accusers. He knew that no one would be able to say that

they had never sinned, no matter how self-righteous they were. Jesus was initiating a model of forgiveness instead of "an eye for an eye."

4. When Jesus saw that there was no one left to condemn the woman, He told her that He would not condemn her, either. Take a moment to appreciate that the one person who could honestly say He had never sinned chose to forgive, not to condemn. He then told her to "go and sin no more." Be sure to emphasize to your group that Jesus was not saying the sin didn't matter, but He was offering the woman forgiveness. He knew that everyone sins, and no sin is worse than another; all that matters is having a repentant heart and not making the same mistakes twice.

5. There is no right answer to this question. Maybe she went back to her family. Maybe she dedicated her life to helping others. Maybe she became one of Jesus' followers as He roamed from town to town teaching.

6. Jesus was not talking about being set free physically, as the people thought He meant. He was really talking about being set free spiritually—free from our sins, free from our mistakes, free from the consequences of what others have done to us, free from emotional problems, free from addiction, etc. If we are true followers of Christ, the only thing that should have control in our lives is the Holy Spirit.

7. The truth that sets us free is nothing other than Jesus Himself, that He came to earth to die for our sins. The point is really brought home in John 3:16, probably one of the most well-known verses in the Bible: "For God so loved the world that he gave his one and only Son, that whoever believes in him shall not perish but have eternal life" (NIV). This is the truth that, if we believe in it, will erase all our past and give us hope for the future.

8. If you live in sin, you are serving the master of sin, Satan. Sin has a way of entangling you and not letting you go, so you continue sinning and therefore are a slave to sin. This is different from being a son of God, because as a son (or daughter) you are free to serve Him out of love.

9. Answers may vary, but should include examples of healthy behavior that can replace particular sins each woman is dealing with.

Chapter 4: Under His Wings

Focus: The truth is that God has promised He will not give us more than we can bear.

1. Answers may vary, but almost all of us have experienced times in our lives when we felt as if we couldn't go on. God is always willing to listen and, just like He gave Elijah, will give us exactly what we need to keep us going. By telling Him our problems, we should feel confident that He will take care of them.

2. Obviously, the job of the shepherd is to care for his sheep. Sheep are stupid creatures that get themselves in trouble often, and the shepherd must always be vigilant in order to keep them from harming themselves. Many times a shepherd cares for hundreds of sheep at a time, but he recognizes each one of them. He feeds them, gives them water, and fights off enemies of the sheep. God does the same for us, and this aspect of His character should help us trust Him. Just as a shepherd would never do anything to harm his sheep, God always wants the best for us.

3. Answers may vary. Each person differs in their definition of restfulness. Some of us are restored through the hustle and bustle of people around us; others require peace and alone time.

4. Answers may vary, but keep in mind that the rod and staff are two tools a shepherd uses to keep his sheep in line. The rod is a stick with a knob on the end that can be used to guide the sheep and in defense against predators, and a staff is a stick with a crook on the end that is used to scoop up sheep when they are in precarious positions. God's rod and staff can be comforting to us because we know He will use them for our protection, and they will give us boundaries.

5. Answers may vary depending on the person. Some people may find more comfort in dwelling in the house of the Lord, while others could appreciate an overflowing cup. Ask each woman to explain her answer.

6. Answers may vary, but dwelling in the "secret place of the Most High" should indicate comfort, security, and care from our loving Father.

7. Answers may vary, but many people have probably experienced situations in which their troubles take them beyond just feeling overwhelmed. Fear is an easy thing to succumb to, and can take many forms—fear of death, fear of someone harming you, fear of facing the day without a former addiction or without someone who used to be in your life. But this psalm speaks of God's protection and watchful care over us. Ask the women to explain when they have experienced fear, and what specific verse in this passage gives them comfort.

8. Answers may vary.

Chapter 5: The Buck Stops Here

Focus: The truth is that we must make the conscious decision to change in order to keep from passing on the same legacy of pain and sin that was given to us.

1. Joseph was favored by his father above all of his brothers, and he even received a brightly colored coat as a token of that love. Not only that, but he also told his brothers that he had had a dream in which all of them were bowing down before him. Everyone would respond differently to this situation, but common reactions would be jealousy, passive-aggressive gossiping about that person, hostility, and even outright anger or rage.

2. Because of the brothers' jealousy, they first decided to kill Joseph and tell their father that a wild animal had eaten him. When Reuben, one of the brothers, disagreed, they compromised and said they would just throw him into a cistern. Against Reuben's knowledge, the other brothers decided to sell Joseph into slavery to the Egyptians. Notice the different responses: most of the brothers were happy with their profit; Reuben tore his clothes and worried what he would tell his father; and the father was so grieved that he refused to be comforted.

3. Joseph took responsibility for his actions, independent of the circumstances he was going through. Because the Lord was with him and he chose to act righteously, he was successful in all of his endeavors, from being in charge of everything Potiphar had to rising in favor in the eyes of the prison warden.

4. Genesis 45:3 tells us that the brothers were not able to speak because they were so terrified of what Joseph would do to them. Verse 5 shows us Joseph's response: "'And now, do not be distressed and do not be angry with yourselves for selling me here, because it was to save lives that God sent me ahead of you'" (NIV).

5. Answers may vary, but many people in Joseph's position would be tempted to deal out their own version of "payback" instead of offering forgiveness. When Joseph told his brothers, "Because it was to save lives that God sent me ahead of you" (NIV), he showed his belief that God brings good out of bad situations. He could have chosen to focus on all of the negative things that he had endured as a result of his brothers' treachery, but instead he focused on what God had accomplished through his situation.

6. The list should include: carts, provisions for the brothers' journey to bring their father back to Egypt, new clothing, and three hundred shekels of silver and five sets of clothes for Benjamin. For his father Joseph sent ten donkeys with the finest things Egypt had to offer, ten female donkeys, and food for the journey.

7. Our sinful nature's first response is to want justice and vengeance toward people who have wronged us. But if we try to seek justice on our own terms, we end up continuing a sinful legacy. If we instead offer forgiveness, then there is no "feed for the fire," so to speak, and hopefully the metaphorical fire of anger, hurt, and persecution will die out.

8. Answers may vary, but could include fixing a hot meal and taking it to the person's house along with a note that tells them you forgive them, offering to pick their kids up from school, and doing other kind things that you know in your heart Jesus would want you to do.

Chapter 6: Forgive with Both Hands

Focus: While we have received forgiveness as a free blessing and an undeserved gift from God, it is also the biggest challenge of our lives that God asks us to turn right around and offer this same forgiveness to others.

1. Answers may vary. While we have hopefully matured as we've grown older and therefore find it easier to forgive, the situations that need

forgiving tend to also grow more serious, and therefore it makes it harder to forgive. See what your group thinks about this.

2. Answers may vary, but excuses could include the level of scarring (physical or emotional) that has taken place because of the wrongdoing, the terrible consequences that have come about because of the other person, or even just the fact that the person hurt your feelings and you're not ready to get over it yet.

3. They made Jesus carry a cross, crucifixion being the death used for the worst criminals; He was crucified along with other criminals; they divided His clothes by casting lots; they sneered at Him; they told Him to save Himself if He was really the Son of God; they mocked Him; as a joke, they posted a written notice above His head that said, "This is the King of the Jews."

4. Jesus cried out to God, requesting, "Father, forgive them, for they do not know what they do" (verse 34).

5. Answers may vary. Spend some time talking about times in your lives when you were the unmerciful servant, refusing to forgive even though you have been forgiven by God the Father.

6. We all deserve the punishment that the unmerciful servant received from his master, but God in His mercy forgives our debts. When we refuse to act toward others as He acted toward us, however, He revokes this mercy and gives us the punishment we justly deserve.

7. Answers may vary.

Chapter 7: True Reconciliation

Focus: Why would we want to reopen scars from our past? Because a mended relationship is where true joy and restoration begin!

1. Answers will vary.

2. Answers will vary, but ask your group to explain why they circled the numbers they did, and see if anyone would volunteer to explain their situation.

3. Verse 19 tells us that because of Christ, God is "not counting men's sins against them" (NIV)—the definition of reconciliation. Since Christ has given us the ministry of reconciliation, we should no longer count men's sins against them, either. This means that if someone does wrong directed toward us, we have a responsibility not to count that against them.

4. Answers may vary, but common reasons for not telling people about Jesus include being embarrassed, not wanting to push people into something they may not want to do, not wanting to appear like a "religious fanatic," or even not having the time.

5. 1) Show him or her what they have done wrong, but keep it between the two of you (which means not gossiping about it to your friends and family!); 2) If he or she does not listen, take two or three other people with you to confront the person; 3) If he or she continues to ignore you, tell the church about the problem (assuming the person is a member of your church); 4) If he or she still does not listen, leave them alone in their sin for fear of being dragged down with them.

6. Answers may vary, but common ways of dealing with difficult situations are getting mad at the person to their face, gossiping about what that person did behind their back, and writing them off as a friend or family member without ever giving them a chance to explain themselves.

7. We must speak truthfully to our neighbors—i.e., family members, friends, and even strangers—which means not being passive-aggressive, not lying to them, and not speaking about them behind their backs. When we are angry, it is easy to lose control of your emotions and actions, but we must be careful not to do anything displeasing to God, no matter how angry we are.

8. Answers will vary, but could include replacing negative thoughts with positive thoughts, taking anger-management classes (depending on the level at which you experience anger), trying to see the wrongdoing from the wrongdoer's point of view, etc.

Chapter 8: Even When It's Not Fair

Focus: As much as we may want to wallow in our own suffering, the truth is that everyone goes through it. Suffering is as old as sin itself.

1. Answers will vary. A couple of examples could be a woman losing her child because a person was driving drunk, a child being abused by his or her parents, or a guilty murderer not being convicted because of insufficient evidence.

2. Answers will vary.

3. The first verse of Job tells us that he was "blameless and upright, and one who feared God and shunned evil." While we do not know why God would continue to let bad things happen to Job, the book of Job tells us that God knew he could handle it, and He wanted to prove to Satan that His servant would remain faithful through it all. He probably also wanted Job to draw all of his strength from God, instead of from his wealth and happy life.

4. Enemies killed all of his oxen and servants, fire consumed his sheep and other servants, other enemies stole all of his camels and killed his servants, and a great wind struck the house of his oldest son and killed all of Job's children and their families. Through all of this torment (and this isn't all of it! Continue reading Job to see what else happens to him), Job never sinned or blamed God. Ask the women in your group to give specific examples of how they might react if they lost their entire family, their savings, and their livelihood.

5. Answers will vary.

6. Answers may vary, but the point of the question is to help people realize that God's timing is not our timing, and God does not promise that we will have a pain-free life.

7. We should store up treasures in heaven, not on earth, because heavenly treasures are eternal and things on earth are only fleeting. When unfair things happen to us, we must remember that we are only on earth for a short time, and we must keep our eyes on the goal of heaven.

Chapter 9: The Power of Joy

Focus: The truth is, if we can learn how to apply joy liberally in our lives, that is how we will truly be set free.

1. Answers will vary, but have fun with this question! Imagine being able to go to your local drugstore or makeup counter and buy a product that automatically makes you a better Christian. What would you want it specifically to do?

2. Answers will vary.

3. Desires of the Sinful Nature: sexual immorality, impurity, debauchery, idolatry, witchcraft, hatred, discord, jealousy, fits of rage, selfish ambition, dissensions, factions, envy, drunkenness, and orgies. Fruits of the Spirit: love, joy, peace, patience, kindness, goodness, faithfulness, gentleness, self-control.

4. In order to bear fruit, we must remain in Christ, which means following Him, acting as He would act, and learning His ways. We can do nothing on our own. We must remain plugged in to the force that feeds us.

5. Abiding, or remaining, means staying plugged into Christ—studying His Word, praying about your circumstances, and spending time talking to Him.

6. Christ is telling us this in order to show us how we can receive joy. If we abide in Christ and obey His commands, His love and joy will be with us. Not only that, but joy will grow in our lives as a fruit of the Spirit.

7. Answers will vary.

Chapter 10: Joy in Suffering

Focus: The truth is, suffering and joy can go hand in hand because suffering is not the end of the story. Joy is the end of the story.

1. Answers will vary, but many people have a difficult time praising God in the midst of trying circumstances. Ask the women in your group to take you through the process of their emotions during that circumstance.

2. Answers may vary, but ways in which members of your group could respond include taking someone to lunch who is experiencing a hard time, mentoring women who want to grow spiritually, and even volunteering at a crisis clinic for women so they could share their own experiences with others.

3. Answers will vary, but this verse should be a comfort to the women as they realize that Christ has undergone the same sufferings we go through, and because of that, He can understand our pain and minister to us. In the same way, we should use our experiences to identify and minister with other people.

4. Happiness is situational and indicates uplifted emotions; but on the other hand, happiness can come and go within moments. It is not a permanent state. However, if you are grounded in Jesus, you can say "it is well with my soul" in whatever situation you are in. It is a "soul thing," not an "emotion thing."

5. We shouldn't be surprised because we are called to follow Christ, and if He endured suffering, then so will we. But we will also participate in His glory once we get to heaven.

6. This passage goes against our human nature, for it tells us that those who are insulted are really blessed, and those who suffer should praise God. This is similar to Jesus' Sermon on the Mount when He teaches the Beatitudes: blessed are the poor in spirit, for they will inherit the Kingdom of God; blessed are those who mourn, for they will be comforted; blessed are the meek, for they will inherit the earth, etc. Jesus' teachings turn the way we view the world upside down and give us entirely different standards to live by.

7. Answers will vary. "Counting" it all joy is the same as considering everything you go through as joyful. Help your group figure out if they do this on a regular basis.

8. Answers will vary.

Chapter 11: Joyful for Others

Focus: The truth is, in order to receive joy in the first place, we must focus on others instead of ourselves.

1. Answers may vary.

2. Answers will vary, but ask the women in your group to think of the different people in their lives. Is any one of them in need? Ask them to think of the different things in which they are involved. Is there an opportunity within any of these situations to edify and minister to others? If they don't have anyone to help or avenues in which to get involved, then challenge them to look for such an opportunity.

3. Answers will vary, but this passage tells us that Christ expects us to not only help our friends, but also our enemies. We should love them, help them, and lend to them without expecting to get anything in return.

4. Because we are Christians and have the Holy Spirit residing within us, we should be able to rise above our personal feelings and act as Christ would act—in other words, be the bigger person. What Jesus asks us to do in this passage is not easy and goes against our very nature, but it is a sign of spiritual maturity to be able to love those who don't love us.

5. This passage tells us that God planned out in advance every day we would ever experience, and He knew about it before we were even conceived! We each have very specific gifts that He has planned for us to use in specific ways for His purposes.

6. Answers may vary, but the point of the question is to reveal that God works everything together for our good—our past, our present, and our future—and He coordinates every detail.

7. God gives us His comfort so we can turn around and give other people the same comfort we have received from Him. God intends for His love, His comfort, and His goodness to be a never-ending cycle. He wants what He gives us to flow directly into the lives of those around us.

Chapter 12: Onward Toward the Goal

Focus: Our job is to forget that which is past and press on toward the goal. There is not one thing on earth we can do that is more important than knowing and loving Jesus as our Lord and Savior, and this should always be our primary focus.

1. Answers will vary, but have fun sharing your exercising experiences with each other.

2. Answers will vary, but share your progress with the group so everyone will feel comfortable sharing with each other.

3. Answers will vary, but some motivating factors could include family members or friends who help you grow spiritually (like this small group!), counselors who have helped you get through tough times, your children who are counting on you, etc.

4. Answers will vary, but the thought of the same Christians who walked with Jesus and wrote His Holy Word, as well as other biblical figures, caring about our spiritual journey should be an inspiring thought. But answers could also include deceased family members, friends, and other respected Christians.

5. Answers will vary, but have each woman give an honest evaluation.

6. Answers will vary. You may even want to have the women pair up and give each other a short assessment, kind of like a sports commentator. But

remind each woman to strive for greatness in order to leave the best legacy they can—a legacy befitting our Savior.

7. Answers will vary, but be honest with each other. Encourage one another as you share your particular burden.

8. Answers will vary.